DANCE ME TO THE END OF LOVE

POEM BY LEONARD COHEN
PAINTINGS BY HENRI MATISSE

EDITED BY LINDA SUNSHINE
A GREG/CLARK DESIGN

A WELCOME BOOK
DISTRIBUTED BY
STEWART, TABORI & CHANG

Dance me to your beauty
with a burning violin

Dance me through the panic

till I'm gathered safely in

Lift me like an olive branch

    and be my homeward dove

Dance me to the end of love

Let me see your beauty

when the witnesses are gone

Let me feel you moving

like they do in Babylon

Show me slowly

what I only

know the limits of

Dance me to
the end of love

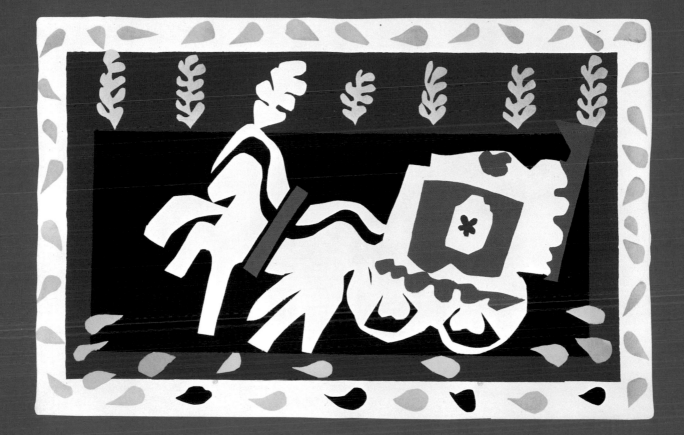

Dance me to the wedding now

dance me on
        and on

H.MATISSE 52

Dance me very tenderly and

dance me very long

We're both of us beneath our love

we're both of us above

Dance me to

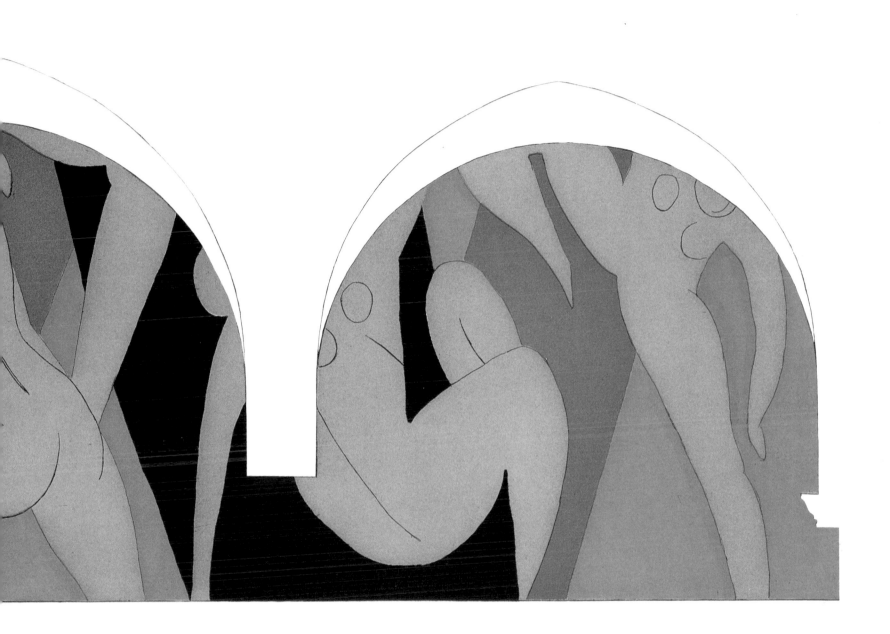

the end of love

Dance me to the children
    who are asking to be born

Dance me through
the curtains

that our kisses have outworn

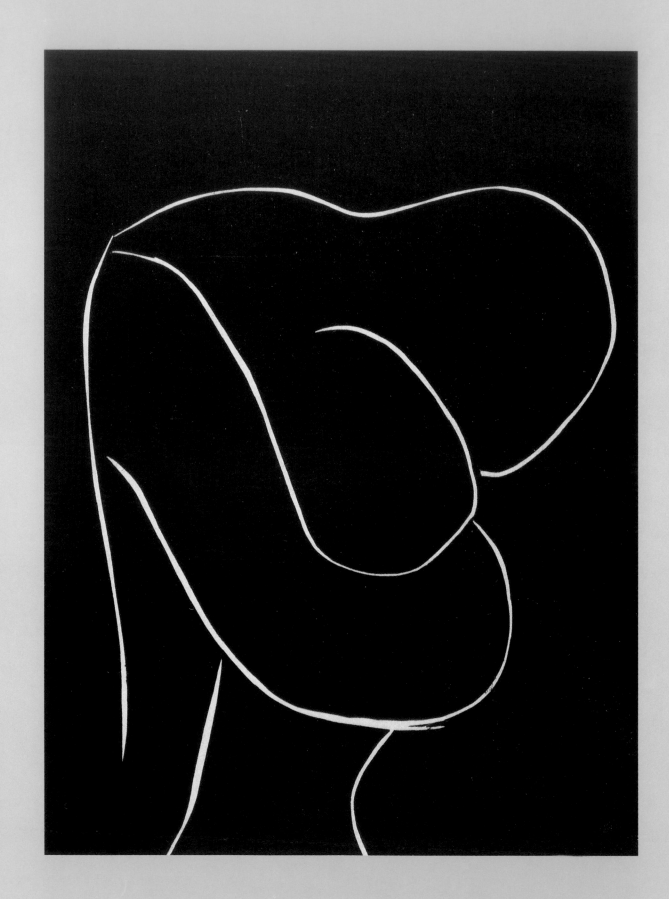

Raise a tent of shelter now
though every thread is torn

Dance me to the end of love

Dance me to your beauty
       with a burning violin

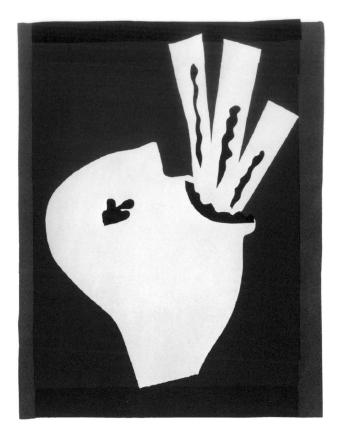

Dance me
through the panic

till I'm gathered
safely in

Touch me with your naked hand
touch me with your glove

Dance me to the end of love

DANCE ME TO THE END OF LOVE

BY LEONARD COHEN

Dance me to your beauty
with a burning violin
Dance me through the panic
till I'm gathered safely in
Lift me like an olive branch
and be my homeward dove
Dance me to the end of love

Let me see your beauty
when the witnesses are gone
Let me feel you moving
like they do in Babylon
Show me slowly what I only
know the limits of
Dance me to the end of love

Dance me to the wedding now
dance me on and on
Dance me very tenderly and
dance me very long
We're both of us beneath our love
we're both of us above
Dance me to the end of love

Dance me to the children
who are asking to be born
Dance me through the curtains
that our kisses have outworn
Raise a tent of shelter now
though every thread is torn
Dance me to the end of love

Dance me to your beauty
with a burning violin
Dance me through the panic
till I'm gathered safely in
Touch me with your naked hand
touch me with your glove
Dance me to the end of love

LEONARD COHEN

*When it comes to lamentations
I prefer Aretha Franklin
to, let's say, Leonard Cohen
He hears a different drum.*

—LEONARD COHEN
"A Different Drum"

Leonard Norman Cohen was born in Montreal in 1934. He attended McGill University where at seventeen he formed a country-and-western trio called The Buckskin Boys. His first collection of poetry, *Let Us Compare Mythologies* (1956), was published while Cohen was still an undergraduate. His second collection, *The Spice Box of Earth*, followed in 1961.

After a brief stint at Columbia University in New York, Cohen left North America, as he wrote, "for an education in the world." He traveled throughout Europe and eventually settled on the Greek island of Hydra. "Greece is a good place/to look at the moon, isn't it" he asked in the poem, "Days of Kindness."

In the mid-1960s, he wrote another collection of poetry, the controversial *Flowers for Hitler*, and two highly acclaimed novels, *The Favourite Game* and *Beautiful Losers*. His most recent anthology of poems, prose and songs, *Stranger Music*, was published in 1993.

He is best known, however, for his music, having made eleven albums including *Various Positions*, *I'm Your Man* and, most recently, *The Future*. His songs—including the seminal 1960s anthem "Suzanne"—have been recorded by artists as diverse as Joan Baez, Neil Diamond, Diana Ross, Rita Coolidge and Joe Cocker. In 1987, Jennifer Warnes released *Famous Blue Raincoat*, an album composed entirely of Cohen's work. Last year, a number of contemporary recording artists collaborated on an evocative tribute to Leonard Cohen in *I'm Your Fan*, an eighteen-song collection featuring R.E.M., John Cale, Ian McCulloch, Pixies, and The House of Love. Cohen's music has also inspired a range of artists from Nick Cave to the late Kurt Cobain of Nirvana who sang: "Give me a Leonard Cohen afterworld" on his eerily prescient recording, "Pennyroyal Tea."

For a man who only "aspired to be a minor poet," Leonard Cohen has produced a prestigious body of work with tremendous appeal for several generations of fans. With the release of *The Future* and the publication of *Stranger Music*, he continues to document maturity and survival while remaining an intensely private and sincerely humble artist. As he wrote in "The Tower of Song":

My friends are gone and my hair is grey.
I ache in the places I used to play.
And I'm crazy for love but I'm not coming on.
I'm just paying my rent every day in the tower of song.

HENRI MATISSE

I had this dance within me
for a long time . . .

—HENRI MATISSE

Henri-Emile-Benoît Matisse was born on New Year's Eve of 1869 in the wool-manufacturing town of Le Cateau-Cambrésis on Flanders Field. At twenty, while working as a law clerk, he was stricken with acute appendicitis and, during his convalescence, was given a box of paints by his mother. "The moment I had this box of colors in my hands," he later remembered, "I had the feeling that my life was there."

He gave up the law and returned to Paris to study painting. In 1896 he exhibited his work in a group show and had his first solo show in 1904. The following year, he was part of the historic group show at the Salon d'Automne where he and his fellow painters were dubbed *les fauves* ("the wild beasts"). "They have thrown a can of paint in the face of the public," declared the critic Camille Mauclair in *Le Matin*. Graffiti on the walls of Montparnasse warned: "Matisse makes you crazy. Matisse is worse than absinthe." Because of such notoriety, however, Matisse began to earn a living from sales of his work.

He purchased a house and studio in Issy-les-Moulineaux, a suburb of Paris, where he sold his work to such patrons as the American millionaire Dr. Albert C. Barnes and the Russian collectors, Ivan Morosov and Sergei Shchukin. In 1925 he was awarded the medal of the Legion of Honor. In 1927, the Carnegie Prize assured him world-wide recognition.

"For fifty years, I have not stopped working for a single moment," he once wrote. "My first session is from nine till twelve. Then I eat, have a short after-lunch nap, and at two pick up my brush again and work until the evening."

A career that began during a convalescence came full circle years later when another operation forced him to stay in bed. Too weak to paint, he cut out and pasted pieces of painted paper, crystallizing memories of the circus, fairy tales and travels into vivid images annotated with such phrases as: "My curves are not crazy." Instead of terminating his artistic career, he began a new one.

A few years later, too ill even to work with scissors, Matisse looked up from his sick bed and noticed the white surface of his ceiling. Attaching a piece of charcoal to a fishing pole, he began drawing figures while laying flat on his back.

In one of his last letters (to Rouveyre, a longtime friend), he wrote, "I hope the survival of my works is guaranteed, as you assure me . . . I never think about it, because I have thrown my ball to the best of my ability; I can no longer certify that it will land on the earth or in the sea or even over the edge from which nothing ever returns."

On November 3rd, 1954, at the age of eighty-five, Henri Matisse died of a heart attack. In 1992, nearly 900,000 people attended a retrospective of his work at The Museum of Modern Art in New York City, making it the largest show in MOMA's history.

Published in 1995 by Welcome Enterprises, Inc.
575 Broadway, New York, NY 10012
Distributed by Stewart, Tabori & Chang, Inc.
575 Broadway, New York, NY 10012
Distributed in Canada by General Publishing Co., Ltd.
30 Lesmill Road, Don Mills, Ontario, Canada M3B 2T6
Distributed in the U.K. by Hi Marketing
38 Carver Road, London SE24 9LT, England
Distributed in Australia and New Zealand by Peribo Pty Limited
38 Beaumont Road, Mount Kuring-Gai NSW 2080, Australia

Library of Congress Cataloging-in-Publication Data
Cohen, Leonard, 1934–
    Dance me to the end of love / poem by Leonard Cohen ; paintings by
Henri Matisse.
    p.   cm.
    ISBN 1-55670-406-2
    I. Love poetry, Canadian.   I. Matisse, Henri, 1869–1954.
II. Title.
PR9199.3.C57D36   1995
811' .54--dc20   94-44504
                                                        CIP

ILLUSTRATION CREDITS:
Front Cover: *Dance (first version)*. Paris, March 1909. Oil on canvas, 102 1/2
x 153 1/2 inches. The Musuem of Modern Art, New York. Gift of Nelson
A. Rockefeller in honor of Alfred H. Barr, Jr. Photo: © 1994 The Museum
of Modern Art, New York.
Back Cover: *Large Reclining Nude*, formerly, *The Pink Nude*. Nice, April–
October 1935. Oil on canvas, 26 x 36 1/2 inches. The Baltimore Museum
of Art. The Cone Collection, formed by Dr. Claribel Cone and Miss Etta
Cone of Baltimore, Maryland.
Page 3: *Music (sketch)*. Collioure, June–July 1907. Oil and charcoal on canvas,
29 x 24 inches. The Museum of Modern Art, New York. Gift of A.
Conger Goodyear in honor of Alfred H. Barr, Jr. Photo: © 1994 The
Museum of Modern Art, New York.
Page 4: *The Sorrow of the King*, 1952. Gouache, cut and pasted, 115 x 156
inches. Musée National d'Art Moderne, Centre Georges Pompidou, Paris.
Photo: Erich Lessing/Art Resource, NY.
Page 5: *Le rêve* (The Dream). Nice, April-May 1935. Oil on canvas, 31 7/8 x
25 5/8 inches. Musée National d'Art Moderne, Centre Georges Pompidou,
Paris. Photo: Art Resource, NY.
Page 6: *Leda and the Swan*, 1944–5. Oil on wood panel, 72 x 61 7/8 inches.
Private Collection, Paris.
Page 7: *Dance II*, 1910. Oil on canvas, 101 3/8 x 153 1/2 inches. The
Hermitage Museum, St. Petersburg.

Page 8–9: *Large Reclining Nude*, 1935. The Baltimore Museum of Art.
See "Back Cover."
Page 10: *Little Dancer on Red Ground*, 1938. Paper cutout with pins, 14 5/8 x
7 1/2 inches. Photo: Robert Miller Gallery, New York.
Page 11: *Danseuses, de la série "Danseuses acrobates"* (Acrobatic Dancers),
1931–2. Lithograph in red chalk. From top: 16 15/16 x 13 3/8 inches; 15 x
11 5/8 inches; 14 1/2 x 13 5/16 inches. Bibliothèque Nationale, Paris.
Page 12: *Blue Nude Jumping Rope*, 1952. Gouache, cut and pasted, 57 1/8 x
38 5/8 inches.
Page 13: *L'enterrement de Pierrot*. Illustration for *Jazz*, 1943. Gouache, cut and
pasted, 17 1/2 x 26 inches. Ecole des Beaux Arts, Paris. Photo: Giraudon/
Art Resource, NY.
Page 14 (Left): *Acrobates* (Acrobats), 1952. Gouache on paper, cut and pasted,
and charcoal on white paper, 83 3/4 x 82 1/2 inches. Private collection.
(Right): *Le chevelure* (The Flowing Hair), 1952. Gouache on paper, cut and
pasted, on white paper, 42 1/2 x 31 1/2 inches. Private collection.
Page 15: *Nu bleu (I)* (Blue Nude I), 1952. Gouache on paper, cut and
pasted, on white paper, 41 3/4 x 30 3/4 inches. Beyeler Collection, Basel.
Page 16: *La Conversation* (The Conversation), 1912. Oil on canvas, 69 5/8 x
85 3/8 inches. The Hermitage Museum, St. Petersburg.
Page 17: *". . . emportés jusqu'aux constellations . . ."*, from *Pasiphaé: Chant de Minos (Les
Crétois)* by Henri de Montherlant, published in 1944. Linoleum cut, 12 7/8 x
9 3/4 inches. The Museum of Modern Art, New York. The Louis E. Stern
Collection. Photo: © 1994 The Museum of Modern Art, New York.
Pages 18–19: *Dancing Figures (3 Spandrel Designs for Barnes Foundation
Mural)*, 1935–6. Etching and color aquatint, 9 5/16 x 29 3/16 inches. The
Baltimore Museum of Art. The Cone Collection, formed by Dr. Claribel
Cone and Miss Etta Cone of Baltimore, Maryland.
Page 20: *Vierge et enfant sur fond étoilé* (Virgin and child on starry background),
1950–1. Lithograph, 12 1/8 x 9 5/8 inches. Bibliothèque Nationale, Paris.
Page 21 (Top): *Interior with a Violin Case*, 1918–9. Oil on canvas, 28 3/4 x
23 5/8 inches. The Musuem of Modern Art, New York. Lillie P. Bliss
Collection. Photo: © 1994 The Museum of Modern Art, New York.
(Bottom): *Lovers Entwined*. Illustration for *Florilège des Amours de Ronsard*,
published in 1948.
Page 22: *Etreinte* (Embrace). Nice, 1941 and 1943. From *Pasiphaé: Chant de
Minos (Les Crétois)* by Henri de Montherlant, published in 1944. Linoleum
cut, 9 1/2 x 6 3/4 inches. Bibliothèque Nationale, Paris.
Page 23: *Icarus*. Illustration for *Jazz*, 1943. Pochoir with gouache, 17 1/8 x
13 1/2 inches. Ecole des Beaux Arts, Paris. Photo: Giraudon/Art
Resource, NY.
Page 25: *Nude with Oranges*, 1952–3. Gouache on paper, cut and pasted,
brush and ink on white paper, 60 3/4 x 42 1/4 inches. Musée National d'Art
Moderne, Centre Georges Pompidou, Paris. Photo: Erich Lessing/Art
Resource, NY.
Page 26 (Top): *The Sword Swallower*. Illustration for *Jazz*, 1943–44. Paper
cutout with gouache mounted on canvas, 17 x 13 1/2 inches. Ecole des
Beaux Arts, Paris. Photo: Giraudon/Art Resource, NY. **(Bottom):**
". . . fraichie sur des lits de violettes . . .", from *Pasiphaé: Chant de Minos (Les Crétois)*
by Henri de Montherlant, published in 1944. Linoleum cut, 12 7/8 x 9 3/4
inches. The Museum of Modern Art, New York. The Louis E. Stern
Collection. Photo: © 1994 The Museum of Modern Art, New York.
Page 27: *Drawing*. Date and source unknown.
Pages 28–9: *Dance (first version)*, 1909. The Musuem of Modern Art, New
York. *See "Front Cover."*
Page 30: *Self-Portrait*. Copyright © 1995 Leonard Cohen.
Page 31: *Self-Portrait*. Nice, 1918. Oil on canvas, 25 5/8 x 21 1/4 inches.
Musée Matisse, Le Chateau Cambrésis. Photo: Art Resource, NY.

PRINTED IN SINGAPORE BY TIEN WAH PRESS (PTE.) LTD   10   9   8   7   6   5   4   3   2   1